WORLD OF BELIEFS

In the same series:
- Judaism
- Buddhism
- Islam

First published in the United States in 2002
by Peter Bedricks Books, an imprint of
McGrawHill Children's Publishing
8787 Orion Place
Columbus, OH 43240
www.MHkids.com

McGraw-Hill
Children's Publishing
A Division of The **McGraw·Hill** *Companies*

ISBN 0-87226-683-4

Christianity
was created and produced by McRae Books
via de' Rustici, 5 – Florence (Italy)
info@mcraebooks.com

SERIES EDITOR Anne McRae
TEXT Hazel Mary Martell
ILLUSTRATIONS Studio Stalio (Alessandro Cantucci, Fabiano Fabbrucci,
Andrea Morandi), Paola Ravaglia, Gian Paolo Faleschini, Lorenzo Cecchi, Donato
Spedaliere, Daniela Astone
GRAPHIC DESIGN Marco Nardi
LAYOUT Laura Ottina, Adriano Nardi
REPRO Litocolor, Florence
PICTURE RESEARCH Loredana Agosta
Printed and bound in Italy by Nuova G.E.P., Cremona

WORLD OF BELIEFS

Hazel Mary Martell

CHRISTIANITY

PETER BEDRICK BOOKS

TABLE OF CONTENTS

Note – This book shows dates as related to the conventional beginning of our era, or the year 0, understood as the year of Christ's birth. All events dating before this year are listed as BCE, or Before Current Era (ex. 928 BCE). Events dating after the year 0 are defined as CE, or Current Era (ex. 24 CE), wherever confusion might arise.

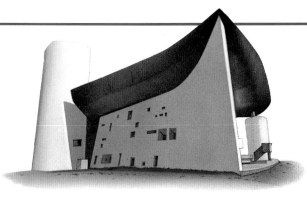

What is Christianity?

Christianity is a religion based on the teachings of Jesus, who was born over 2000 years ago in what is now Israel. His followers believed he was the son of God and they called him Messiah or **Christ,** from the Greek word for Anointed One. They then became known as Christians and their beliefs became known as Christianity. After Jesus died, some of his followers set out on **missionary** journeys, spreading his teachings to others. Today there are Christians in all parts of the world. The cross, on which Jesus died, is the symbol of Christianity, and it also symbolizes life after death.

*This Christian **cross** comes from Turkey, where it was made in the 7th century.*

The Star of David is the symbol of Judaism, the religion into which Jesus was born.

Jesus and Judaism
Jesus lived his life as a Jew, and Christianity has its roots in **Judaism.** However, Judaism teaches that its followers are God's chosen people, while Christians believe that God's love is available to everyone through his son Jesus.

The Holy Trinity
Most Christians believe that God is three separate and equal persons, who are also all joined together as one. Separately they are known as God the Father, God the Son (or Jesus), and God the **Holy Spirit** (or Holy Ghost), while together they are known as the Holy Trinity. The Holy Spirit is thought of as God's power at work in the world and was present as the world was created.

The Holy Spirit is often represented by a white dove, as in this picture of the Holy Trinity.

Christians believe that God the Father created the universe and that Adam and Eve, shown here in the Garden of Eden, were the first people to live on Earth.

God the Creator
Christians, like Jews and Muslims, believe in one God who created the universe and everything in it, including human beings, in six days. They believe that this was an expression of both his power and his love and that everything has its beginning and its ending in God. Christians also believe that the life of Jesus as a human being, followed by his death on the cross, are signs of God's great love for the people of the world he created.

Christian duties

All Christians are expected to obey the **Ten Commandments** (also known as the Decalogue), which God gave to Moses many centuries before Jesus was born. The first of these says that Christians should worship only one God.

This stained glass window shows the Devil trying to tempt Jesus to follow him.

God holds the Greek letters Alpha and Omega, to show that he is the beginning and end of all things.

Some Christians, like these medieval horsemen, travel to places that they consider sacred, such as important churches or shrines.

Human and divine

Before he started teaching others about God, Jesus spent 40 days and 40 nights in the desert. Because Jesus was human as well as divine, the Devil thought he could tempt him away from God by offering him power over all the world. Jesus resisted, but the story reminds Christians that they might still be tempted, even though they believe in God.

A choir leads the congregation in singing hymns in many Christian church services.

These young people are taking part in the Jubilee, a huge pilgrimage to Rome, Italy, that took place in the year 2000.

Music and singing

Christians worship and honor God by informal private prayer and by formal **church** services and ceremonies. As the religion became firmly established, music and singing began to play an important part in the formal services. Traditionally, church music was played on an organ, but many other musical instruments have been used, including the guitar.

In this Italian Renaissance picture, the Archangel Gabriel tells Mary that she will give birth to the Son of God.

The Life of Jesus

There is no accurate story of the life of Jesus, but most historians now agree that he was born in Bethlehem around 5 BCE and spent most of his life in Nazareth. When he was about 30 years old, he began preaching, speaking out against poverty and against the greed and hypocrisy of rich people and priests. The poor loved him, but he made enemies among the Jewish authorities and the Romans who ruled over them. Betrayed by one of his followers, he was put to death as a political rebel.

Adoration of the Magi

At Jesus's birth, three Wise Men, or **Magi**, from the East were guided to Bethlehem by a star. They brought with them gifts of gold, frankincense, and myrrh – symbolizing virtue, prayer, and suffering – to honor Jesus as King, God, and human.

John the Baptist

Around 27 CE John the Baptist, who was Jesus's cousin, began preaching on the banks of the river Jordan and **baptizing** people there. One of them was Jesus and, as John baptized him, the Holy Spirit descended on him in the form of a dove.

The Flight into Egypt

Shortly after Jesus was born, Herod the Great, the Roman ruler of Judaea, ordered all baby boys in Bethlehem to be killed. Herod was afraid of Jesus's power. Jesus survived because his parents fled with him to Egypt.

Jesus's early years

After they returned from Egypt, Mary, Joseph, and the young Jesus settled in Nazareth near Lake Galilee. Joseph worked as a carpenter and Jesus probably followed the same trade until he began preaching when he was about 30.

Left: Baby Jesus with his mother, Mary, and her husband Joseph, who was Jesus's human father, during the flight into Egypt.

Jesus and his Disciples

Jesus spent the last three years of his life teaching people about God's love for them by preaching sermons or by telling simple stories, known as parables. His closest followers were the **Twelve Disciples** or **Apostles**.

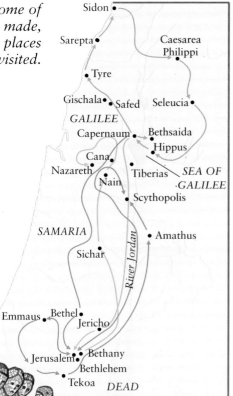

This map shows some of the journeys Jesus made, and the places that he visited.

Palestine in the time of Jesus.

The Last Supper

This mosaic shows Jesus and his Disciples in Jerusalem, eating supper in celebration of the Jewish feast of the Passover. It became known as the **Last Supper** because it was the last time the men ate together before Judas Iscariot, one of the Disciples, betrayed Jesus to the Roman soldiers.

Death and Resurrection

Jesus was sentenced to death by crucifixion (being nailed to a cross). After his death, his body was placed in a tomb and guarded, but three days after his death, Christians believe, Jesus came back to life and escaped from the tomb, in what is known as the **Resurrection**.

*Left: Over the centuries, scenes of the **Crucifixion** and the Resurrection have been painted many times.*

Early Christianity

After the Resurrection, Jesus spent some time on Earth with his Disciples before ascending into Heaven. Before he left, he told them to go on missionary journeys to spread his teachings across the world as they knew it. Peter and the Apostle Paul traveled the farthest, but, although they both reached Rome and **converted** many people on their travels, they both died for their faith and almost 300 years passed before Christianity became the official religion of the vast Roman Empire.

The Acts of the Apostles
Much information about the early spread of Christianity comes from the Acts of the Apostles (above), written by Luke as a sequel to his **gospel**. However, he focuses on the work of Peter and Paul and tells us little about the other Apostles.

The Apostles Peter and Paul helped to spread Christianity after Jesus died.

Saint Peter
Peter and his brother, Andrew, were fishermen on Lake Galilee until Jesus called them to be his Disciples. Peter was the leader of the Disciples and, after Jesus died, he led the Christian community. He is sometimes known as the rock upon which the **Church** was built.

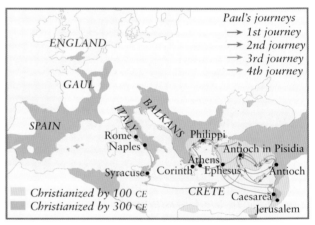

Map: St Paul's journeys and the spread of Christianity.

Early persecutions
As the Christian faith spread, its followers often came into conflict with the ruling Roman authorities, but they probably suffered most under the rule of the Roman emperor Nero. He blamed them for many of his problems, including a disastrous fire in Rome, and had many of them executed.

Some Christians were forced to fight wild animals to entertain the Romans.

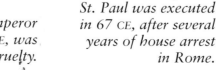

Nero, Roman emperor from 54 to 68 CE, was famous for his cruelty.

Tradition says that St. Paul was executed in 67 CE, after several years of house arrest in Rome.

The early Christians in Rome buried their dead in the catacombs (left), which are narrow, underground passages with burial niches in the walls. They also worshiped there in times of persecution (below).

Worshiping in secret

Unlike the Christians, the Romans worshiped many different gods and believed that their emperors became gods when they died. Everyone was supposed to worship them and those who refused to do so were killed, imprisoned, or forced to become slaves. Christians, who refused to worship the emperor, often had to worship their own god in secret. Some emperors were more tolerant than others, but there were large-scale persecutions in 250, 258, and 303 CE.

Early Christians found ways of making themselves known to other Christians. For example, the word Paternoster (Latin for "Our Father") is carved into this stone in a hidden form.

The emperor Constantine gave the Lateran Palace to the bishop of Rome in 313. He also gave back to the Christians the property which had earlier been taken from them (below).

A gold coin showing the head of the Roman emperor Constantine I.

Acceptance of Christianity

Constantine the Great was acclaimed Roman emperor in the West in 306 CE, but his position was not secure until 312 CE when he defeated his rival Maximentius at the Battle of the Milvian Bridge. Tradition says that before the battle he saw a vision of the Christian cross with the words, "In this sign, conquer." After his victory, he accepted Christianity, and during his reign he made it the official religion of the Roman Empire.

The Church

The word church has two different meanings for Christians. Originally it was used to describe the whole community of Christians throughout the world. However, as Christianity became firmly established and people no longer had to keep their faith a secret, the word church was also used to describe the buildings in which Christians met to worship and pray. Originally these were simple structures of stone or wood, but gradually they became more elaborate and beautifully decorated.

This mosaic shows a Christian church from the 2nd century CE. Its design was based on the Roman public meeting hall, known as a basilica.

St. Peter's basilica
Once Christianity was accepted as the official religion of the Roman Empire, Rome quickly became its center. St. Peter was recognized as the first bishop of Rome and in 333 CE this basilica was built, possibly on the site of his burial.

It took many years to build a cathedral. This one at Burgos in Spain was started in 1221, but had its towers added in the 15th century.

Cathedrals and bishops
To help it run smoothly, the Christian world was divided up into areas known as dioceses. Every diocese was divided into many smaller parishes, each with its own church and priest. A bishop was in charge of the diocese and, as a symbol of his importance, he sat on a throne known as a "cathedra." From this comes the word **"cathedral,"** meaning the main church in the diocese where the bishop had his seat. Many cathedrals from the Middle Ages still stand today.

During the Middle Ages, carved figures, known as gargoyles, acted as spouts for draining rainwater from the church roofs, and some people believed they scared evil spirits away from the building. This one is on the Cathedral of Notre Dame in Paris.

The use of incense

Long before Christianity, incense was burned in pagan ceremonies. The Three Magi brought frankincense to the baby Jesus as a sign of his divinity, and later it became a symbol of prayer. It was first used in Christian churches in the 6th century CE.

This beautifully decorated censer was used for burning incense during Mass.

Spreading the Word

Spreading the Christian message is an important part of church services. It can be done as readings from the **Bible**, which is often placed on a lectern (left), or as sermons preached from a pulpit.

Church architecture

The earliest churches were built in the style of ancient Roman public buildings, but over the centuries different areas developed their own styles, using stone, brick, or wood. Most large churches were richly decorated, but smaller ones were sometimes quite plain and simple, like this one from Newton Arlush in Cumbria, England (left).

Baptistries

Baptism is the ceremony which brings people into the Christian faith. The first baptisms were done on the banks of rivers. Later they took place in buildings called baptistries, which stood near churches.

Infant baptism

By the Middle Ages, most Christians were baptized as children. The ceremony then took place inside the church around a font (like this one on the left). This contained holy water which the priest poured over the child's head as he named the child.

Above: the baptistry, cathedral, and leaning tower, at Pisa, Italy.

Stories in windows and paintings

For many centuries after Christianity was established, few people could read or write. To help them understand and remember stories from the Bible, scenes from the stories were often depicted in stained glass windows or painted on the inside walls of a church.

Church music

Hymns and music have been part of Christian worship since the late 4th century CE, but the music wasn't written down until the Middle Ages.

Christianity in the Middle Ages

In the early Middle Ages, Christianity began to spread beyond the boundaries of the former Roman Empire. Many people were converted to the faith by missionaries from Ireland and Rome. Others learned of the new beliefs as they traded with people who were already Christians. However, for many years some were Christians in public, but worshiped their old gods in secret.

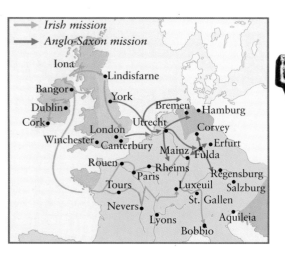

Map showing routes followed by British and Irish missionaries in the early Middle Ages.

Right: The Irish continued to use Celtic designs to decorate copies of the Gospels.

Celtic Christianity

After the Romans left Britain in 410 CE, the Angles, Jutes, and Saxons invaded from the East. They brought their own religions with them, but Christianity survived, especially in Cornwall, Wales, and Ireland. It became known there as Celtic Christianity. The cast-iron plaque of the Crucifixion (below) is from this time.

The circle on the Celtic cross (left) came from a pre-Christian symbol for the sun.

St. Columba

The Irish missionary St. Columba went to the island of Iona in 563 and founded a monastery (below). From there, other missionaries set out to convert the people of Scotland and northern England.

Christianity spread to Scandinavia during the 10th century. The earliest churches in Norway were built of wood and some can still be seen today (right).

St. Augustine's mission

In 596 **Pope** Gregory I sent Augustine, an Italian churchman, to convert the people of England to Christianity. He landed in Kent and Christianity spread out from there. This led to conflict with the Celtic church, but by 768 the Roman church was in control.

The Holy Roman Empire

In 755, Pepin the Short, king of the Franks, saved Rome and the pope from an attack by the Lombards from northern Italy. When the Lombards attacked Rome again in 774, Pepin's son, Charles (who became known as Charles the Great or Charlemagne), marched over the Alps and saved Rome and the pope once more. In gratitude, Pope Leo III crowned Charlemagne emperor of the West on Christmas Day in 800. This was the start of a special relationship (left) between the popes and the rulers of what became known as the Holy Roman Empire. But when Charlemagne's son, Louis the Pious, died in 843, his kingdom was split into three and in 962 the king of Germany was elected Holy Roman Emperor. Between the 11th and 13th centuries, the emperors and the popes vied for control of Europe.

A bronze statue of Charlemagne from the 9th century. Between 771 and 800 he conquered most of the Christian countries of western Europe.

The pope leaves Rome

By the 14th century the relationship between the Holy Roman Empire and the Church had weakened. In 1305 King Phillip IV of France influenced the appointment of a Frenchman as Pope Clement (below). Four years later Clement V moved the papal court from Rome to Avignon in southern France and the next six popes ruled the Church from there. After criticism of the luxury and corruption at Avignon, Pope Gregory XI moved back to Rome in 1377.

The wealth and power of the Holy Roman Empire are symbolized by this 11th century crown and 12th century orb, whose cross shows the empire's link with the Christian Church.

This carving shows Pope Urban VI receiving the papal key from St. Peter in 1378.

The Great Western Schism

Pope Gregory XI died in 1378 and Urban VI was elected in his place. When he tried to curb the power of the cardinals, however, they elected a pope of their own, Clement VII, who went back to Avignon. A period known as the **Great Schism** followed, with the two popes holding rival courts. It was ended in 1417 with the election of Martin V in Rome.

The Crusades

In the 7th century a major new religion, called Islam, developed in Arabia and spread quickly throughout North Africa and the Middle East. Its followers were called Muslims. By 634 they had reached Jerusalem, which was a sacred city to them, as well as to Christians and Jews. People of all three faiths lived together there in relative harmony, but in 1095 Pope Urban II decided to claim Jerusalem for Christians and launched the first of the **Crusades**, fierce military attacks that continued into the next three centuries.

The First Crusade
The knights of the First Crusade captured Jerusalem on July 15, 1099, and killed all the Jews and Muslims they found there. They then took control of a narrow strip of land along the nearby coast, where they captured the cities of Edessa, Antioch, and Tripoli and made them into Crusader kingdoms.

Some knights went on the Crusades because they were religious and thought God would be pleased with them. Others went hoping to make their fortune.

Crusader castles
During their stay in the **Holy Land**, the Crusaders built churches, **monasteries**, and castles in the European style. The most famous castle is Krak des Chevaliers in Syria (above), which was built by the Count of Tripoli. He later sold it to the Knights Hospitalers, a wealthy religious order formed to care for **pilgrims** in Jerusalem, but which had taken on a military role.

London
Paris Verdun
Würtzburg
Tours Vézelay
Regensburg
Vienna
Toulouse
Lyons
Madrid Aigues-Mortes
Genoa Venice Budapest
Lisbon
Marseille Pisa Zara
Rome Spalato
Bari
Brindisi
Tunis Messina Dyrrachium
Constantinople
Nicaea
Black Sea
Mistra Sardi
Rodhes Konya Caesarea
Candia
Edessa
Mediterranean Sea
Antioch
Nicosia
Aleppo
Tripoli
Damietta Acre
Damascus
Jerusalem

Traveling to the Holy Land
As this map shows, the Crusaders set out from many different countries and followed different routes to reach Jerusalem, with some going all the way overland and others crossing the Mediterranean by ship. The journey was often arduous and some Crusaders died of illness and exhaustion along the way.

At this time, new maps of the world appeared with Jerusalem at the center, while circular maps like this one (right) helped pilgrims find their way around the city.

18

The Fourth Crusade

In 1198 the Fourth Crusade was called to fight against the Egyptians, but the army that gathered was very poor and had few weapons or ships. The city of Venice agreed to provide equipment in exchange for help in defeating its trading rival, Constantinople. Among the items brought back from Constantinople were the bronze horses below.

The Crusaders rebuilt the Church of the Holy Sepulchre in Jerusalem.

Pilgrimages to the Holy Land

By the Middle Ages some people in Europe had become quite wealthy and could afford to go on pilgrimages to see the places associated with Jesus's life on Earth. It was a long and difficult journey to the Holy Land, however, and so those who were too sick or too busy to go themselves sometimes paid other people to go for them.

Pilgrims brought back many religious relics from their journeys, including this thorn (left) which is said to have come from the crown of thorns worn by Jesus on the cross.

Saladin (below) was one of Islam's great heroes. Having united the Muslims into a well-organized army, he defeated the Crusaders and in 1192 forced them to return to Europe.

The Islamic armies

Under Saladin's command, the Muslim armies were well-equipped (above) and had a much better system of communication than the Crusaders, using beacon fires, smoke signals, and carrier pigeons. They also built simple forts (left) that were strong and easy to defend.

The end of the Crusades

The Crusades to the Holy Land ended in 1291 after the fall of the Crusader stronghold at Acre, but the fight against the Muslims in Spain continued. The cross on the right is said to have been carried by the eleventh century Spanish warrior, El Cid. Most of his victories were only temporary and parts of Spain remained in Muslim hands until 1492.

The Bible

The Bible is Christianity's most sacred book. It was written between about 1000 BCE and 100 CE and is made up of many different books, divided into the Old and the New Testaments. The writing is said to have been inspired by God, and Christians are encouraged to study the Bible every day. Even nonbelievers see it as a great work of literature containing many interesting stories. The work of Bible societies has ensured that at least some parts of the Bible have been translated into more than 560 languages.

In 1947 archeologists discovered a collection of written scrolls, including many books of the Old Testament, stored in jars and hidden in caves at Qumran near the Dead Sea.

The Dead Sea Scrolls were hidden around 68 CE and so have been valuable for checking the accuracy of other Old Testament texts.

This medieval illustration shows the Creation of the animals.

The Old Testament

The Old Testament makes up the larger part of the Bible. Most of it was written originally in Hebrew and is sacred to Jews as well as Christians. It tells the story of the world, and particularly of the Jewish people, from the Creation to just before the birth of Jesus. Many of its books tell the stories of different prophets, such as Jonah, Daniel, and Isaiah.

The New Testament

The New Testament is the part of the Bible which tells us about the life of Jesus and the events that followed his death. It is much shorter than the Old Testament and has been translated into many more languages. In the nineteenth and twentieth centuries many missionaries used the New Testament to teach people how to read, as well as to teach them about Christianity.

The New Testament begins with the four books of the Gospels. According to Christian tradition they were written by Matthew, Mark, Luke, and John (right).

This diagram shows the arrangement of the books in the Christian Bible.

OLD TESTAMENT
The Law
- GENESIS
- EXODUS
- LEVITICUS
- NUMBERS
- DEUTERONOMY

Books of History
JOSHUA, JUDGES, RUTH, 1 SAMUEL, 2 SAMUEL, 1 KINGS, 2 KINGS, 1 CHRONICLES, 2 CHRONICLES, EZRA, NEHEMIAH, ESTHER

The Wisdom Books
- JOB
- PSALMS
- PROVERBS
- ECCLESIASTES
- SONG OF SONGS

The Prophets
ISAIAH, JEREMIAH, LAMENTATIONS, EZEKIEL, DANIEL, HOSEA, JOEL, AMOS, OBADIAH, JONAH, MICAH, NAHUM, HABAKKUK, ZEPHANIAH, HAGGAI, ZECHARIAH, MALACHI

DEUTERO CANONICAL BOOKS

The early Christian Church took 12 books from the Greek version of the Old Testament which had not been part of the original Hebrew Bible. These books, which are known as the Apocrypha, are not usually printed in Protestant Bibles.

NEW TESTAMENT
Gospels
MATTHEW, MARK, LUKE, JOHN, ACTS

The Letters
ROMANS, 1 CORINTHIANS, 2 CORINTHIANS, GALATIANS, EPHESIANS, PHILIPPIANS, COLOSSIANS, 1 THESSALONIANS, 2 THESSALONIANS, 1 TIMOTHY, 2 TIMOTHY, TITUS, PHILEMON, HEBREWS, JAMES, 1 PETER, 2 PETER, 1 JOHN, 2 JOHN, 3 JOHN, JUDE, REVELATIONS

The story of Jesus's descent into Hell was not told in the four Gospels written by his Disciples, but appeared in the fourth century Gospel of Nicodemus.

St. Jerome's translation

St. Jerome (right) was an Italian scholar who settled in Bethlehem in the fifth century. He is best known for translating the Old Testament from Hebrew into Latin. (Earlier Latin versions were translated from Greek.) His version is known as the Vulgate Bible. It became the official version for the Roman Catholic church and later English versions were based on it.

Producing books by hand

Until the fifteenth century, all books were copied out by hand onto parchment or vellum, which was made from animal skin. Sometimes the whole Bible was copied, but more often just the Gospels were written out. They were usually illustrated in color and decorated with gold and silver, then bound in beautiful covers.

The first printers

The first printed books were produced page by page from woodcuts. This was slow and expensive, but in 1450 the German craftsman Johannes Gutenberg invented a different printing method that used individual letters on movable type that could be used again and again.

Johannes Gutenberg first used his printing press to print the Bible. He then printed other books.

The whole Bible has been translated into over 560 languages and is probably one of the world's most widely read books.

The Reformation and the Bible

For many centuries the Bible was only available in Latin translations. Most ordinary people could not read it for themselves, so they had to rely on priests and scholars to explain it to them. From the early sixteenth century, however, scholars started to translate the Bible into other languages. The 1534 edition above was translated into German by Martin Luther, the priest whose ideas led to the **Reformation** (see pages 26–27).

The Orthodox Church

As Christianity became established throughout the former Roman Empire, different groups of people interpreted Jesus's teachings in different ways. Some differences could be resolved, but others led to splits in the Church which have lasted to the present day. The first major split developed in the first millennium between the Church in the former Western Empire, based in Rome, and the Church in the former Eastern Empire, based in Constantinople and known as the Orthodox church.

Icons with scenes of people or events from the Bible, or from the lives of the saints, are very important in the Orthodox church. Many are decorated with gold and silver.

Constantinople
The city of Constantinople (right) was the heart of the Byzantine empire. It had many Christian churches, including Hagia Sophia, which was completed in 537.

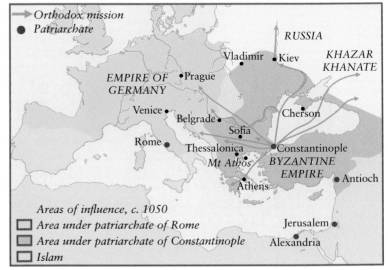

The beautiful church of Hagia Sophia in Constantinople was the center of Christianity in the East. It later became a mosque and is now a museum.

Right: Orthodox beliefs spread out quickly from Constantinople.

Orthodox mission
● Patriarchate

RUSSIA

Vladimir ● Kiev

KHAZAR KHANATE

EMPIRE OF GERMANY ● Prague

Venice ● Belgrade ● Cherson

Sofia

Rome ● Thessalonica Constantinople

Mt Athos BYZANTINE EMPIRE

Athens ● Antioch

Areas of influence, c. 1050
☐ Area under patriarchate of Rome
☐ Area under patriarchate of Constantinople
☐ Islam

Jerusalem ●

Alexandria

The East-West schism
The two figures on this ivory diptych (left) personify Rome and Constantinople. They represent the East-West schism in the Church, which occurred in 1054 when the differences between the two became too great to resolve. The Orthodox church refused to accept the pope in Rome as its head any longer.

The Coptic Orthodox church

The Egyptian Christians, known as Copts, split away from Rome in the middle of the 6th century because they did not believe that Jesus was human as well as divine. Apart from this belief, however, they have much in common with the Orthodox church, including using icons like the one below.

Greek Orthodox

St. Paul established the Christian church in Greece on one of his missionary journeys in the 1st century. Greece was then part of the Roman Empire, and it became part of the Byzantine (or Eastern Roman) Empire in 395. In 1453 this empire was conquered by the Ottomans, who were Muslims, but Orthodox Christianity survived in Greece.

St. George, the patron saint of England, is also very popular in the Slavic lands. Above, an icon of St. George slaying the dragon.

Greek Orthodox priests usually have beards and wear their hair long.

This Orthodox Christian church is in Albania.

Vladimir I's sons Boris and Gleb (below) were the first Russian saints.

(Right) The baptism of Vladimir I, Grand Prince of Kiev and Novgorod, in 988.

The Russian Orthodox crucifix has three crossbars.

Russian Orthodox

The Russian Orthodox church was founded in 988 after Vladimir I decided that his state needed a major religion. He asked for reports on Islam, Judaism, and Roman and Byzantine (or Orthodox) Christianity. Orthodox Christianity impressed him the most and he even decided to marry the Byzantine emperor's sister, Anna.

23

Monastic Life

As early as 305, St. Anthony of Egypt had devised a way of organizing the Christian **hermits** in his country into a monastic community living according to certain rules. They continued to live separately, but in 318 Pachomius, another Egyptian, founded the first monastery where monks lived together. Monasticism then spread northward and westward, and both men and women took vows of poverty, chastity, and obedience. They devoted their lives to prayer and work, including teaching, looking after the sick, and helping the poor.

Life in a monastery
A monk at a monastery such as Cluny (left) went to prayers at various times of the day and night in the church, which was the biggest and most important building on the site. The rest of the time was spent reading or copying religious books, or working in the surrounding fields and vegetable gardens that provided food and drink for the monastery.

Monastic orders
Many different orders of monks and nuns were established in the West. The earliest were the Benedictines, who led a life of private prayer within their monasteries. The Cistercians and the Carthusians were similar but stricter orders. Later orders included the Franciscans and the Dominicans who spent time doing charitable work in the outside world.

St. Francis (far left) founded the Franciscan monastic order and St. Clare (left) founded the Poor Clares.

St. Benedict (above) put together a set of rules for monastic life in the 6th century.

Nuns and convents

Women who wanted to devote their lives to Christianity were known as nuns, and they lived in convents or nunneries which were usually separate from monasteries. Not all women entered convents for religious reasons, however. For example, some were sent for refusing to obey their fathers or husbands, while others went because they had lost their homes.

The Beguine sisters in Belgium and Holland live religious lives, but do not take vows.

Greek Orthodox monasteries

Monasticism is very important in the Greek Orthodox religion and Mount Athos is its Holy Mountain. Monks first went there in 962 and by the 11th century there were 180 monasteries on the site. No women and no female animals were allowed, and each monk was given a knotted cord, rather than rosary beads like the ones on the left, to help him to pray.

One of the 20 present-day monasteries on Mount Athos in northeastern Greece.

Hermits

The first people to lead a religious life cut off from the rest of the world were the hermits who lived alone in the wilderness in the early years of Christianity. Some lived in caves, but others spent their lives on top of rocks or pillars. The isolation drove some of them crazy, but even after monasteries were built, some religious people preferred to live as hermits.

The Reformation

By the end of the 15th century, new ideas about life and religion were spreading across Europe, helped by an increase in printed books and papers. Some people began to think that the Catholic church had grown too powerful and corrupt, as some popes gave important jobs to their friends and family in exchange for valuable gifts, and allowed people to buy forgiveness for their sins. Many felt the Church should be reformed and improved, but instead their efforts led to the formation of a new group, known as the **Protestants**.

Martin Luther

When the German priest Martin Luther nailed a list of 95 theses, or ideas, for reforming the Church to the church door in Wittenburg in 1517, he intended to improve the Church. Instead he started a split within it.

Not all Protestants agreed with Martin Luther, who is shown below (on the left) with some other Protestant reformers.

Corruption in the Church

Although many people went into the Church because they were sincerely religious, others went for more selfish reasons. The wealth of some monasteries and convents attracted those who wanted a life of luxury, and the rules of chastity and obedience were often ignored.

John Calvin

John Calvin was a Frenchman who had studied law and theology, who became involved in the Protestant movement in the early 1530s. His views were more severe than Luther's. Calvinist churches (above) were very plain, the pulpit was the most important feature, and men and women were made to sit separately.

Henry VIII

King Henry VIII of England disagreed strongly with Martin Luther's ideas, but broke away from the Church in Rome in 1534 when Pope Clement VII refused to annul his marriage to Catherine of Aragon.

Despite making himself Head of the Church of England, Henry VIII remained a Roman Catholic.

Sir Thomas More (1477–1535) became Henry VIII's chancellor in 1529. He was executed for treason after he opposed the king becoming head of the Church in England.

Erasmus

Erasmus was one of the great humanist scholars and teachers of the 16th century. He was respected by all sides, although he condemned the corruption of the Catholic church and was opposed to the Protestant reformers.

Erasmus was born in Rotterdam around 1466.

This map shows how Protestantism (shown in pink and purple) had spread in Europe by 1565.

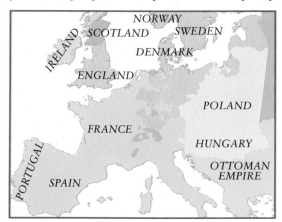

Ignatius Loyola (1491–1556, below) founded the Society of Jesus (or Jesuits) in 1540. He was made a saint in 1622.

The Counter-Reformation

Pope Paul III (below) became pope in 1534. He was so dismayed by the split in the Church, caused by the Protestant movement, that in 1545 he launched the Counter-Reformation to find ways of improving the image of the Catholic church and ridding it of the worst abuses.

The Jesuits

The Jesuits were a monastic order, founded on military lines to promote and expand the Catholic faith. Its members had to promise to go wherever the pope sent them and soon made a name for themselves as teachers and missionaries all over the world.

Art and Christianity

Over the centuries, many different kinds of art have been important in Christianity. Paintings, carvings, stained glass, mosaics, and statues have been used to illustrate stories from the Bible and from the lives of the saints, and to make church buildings as beautiful as possible. Not all branches of the Church agree on what kind of art they will allow, however. For example, the Orthodox church does not allow three dimensional images, such as statues, while many Protestant churches do not allow wall paintings.

This Russian icon of the Old Testament Trinity was painted by Andrey Rublyov (1370–1430).

The altarpiece
On the wall behind the altar in many churches there is either a decorated screen, called a reredos, or a sacred picture or statue, called an altarpiece. The Virgin Mary, also known as the **Madonna**, is a popular image in both the Catholic and the Orthodox churches. She is often portrayed with the baby Jesus in her arms, as in this painting by the Italian artist Giotto.

From 730 to 843 the Byzantine Empire banned icons. Many were destroyed or damaged.

It took hundreds of workers and many years to build a Gothic cathedral.

Map of the main Gothic cathedrals in Europe.

SWEDEN
Abo
Uppsala
Reval
Linköping
Visby
Riga
ENGLAND
DENMARK
York
Lincoln
Canterbury
Lübeck
Exeter
Utrecht
Magdeburg
Salisbury
Münster
Naumburg
Cologne
Amiens
Prague
Chartres
Reims
Worms
Angers
Paris
Vienna
Santiago de Compostela
Bourges
Auxerre
Strasbourg
HOLY
Bordeaux
Toulouse
Basel
ROMAN
Leon
Lyons
Milan
EMPIRE
Burgos
Albi
Genoa
Zaragoza
Avignon
Pisa
Florence
Segovia
Tarragona
Gerona
Siena
Orvieto
Toledo
Barcelona
Rome
SPAIN
Valencia
Palma
ITALY
Origins of Gothic art
Palermo

Patrons of the arts

In the Middle Ages many kings and popes commissioned artists to produce new religious works. For example, the Wilton Diptych (left) was painted for King Richard II of England who also appears on it. One of the most famous is the Sistine Chapel in the Vatican in Rome (right), which has paintings by Botticelli, as well as Michelangelo.

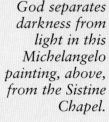

Portraying the wealthy

During the Renaissance, some powerful families commissioned paintings showing themselves under the direct protection of the saints. In the painting on the right by Domenico Ghirlandaio (who also worked on the Sistine Chapel), the Madonna of Mercy is shown protecting members of the Vespucci family.

God separates darkness from light in this Michelangelo painting, above, from the Sistine Chapel.

Mosaics and wall paintings

Pictures, such as this mosaic of Noah releasing the animals from the Ark after the Flood, not only made churches look more beautiful, but also helped people who could not read to understand the stories they were being told. After the Reformation, many of the pictures were destroyed or painted over in those churches that became Protestant.

Calvinists and some other Protestants thought it was wrong to have statues and paintings in churches, and so they destroyed them in big fires.

Embroidery and needlework

Richly patterned tapestries, altar cloths, and kneeling cushions are some of the obvious church items to be decorated with embroidery and other kinds of needlework. In many branches of the Christian Church some of the priests' ceremonial clothes, such as this modern chasuble from Venice that is worn during the Mass, are also embroidered with threads of silk, gold, and silver.

This 20th century church, by French architect Le Corbusier, looks very different from earlier ones.

Wars of Religion

The split in the Church which followed the Reformation led to a time of religious turmoil in western Europe. Thousands of people were killed as each side tried to force its will on the other. During the 16th century most of the struggles were contained within individual countries. However, in 1618 a war started in Protestant Bohemia against its Catholic ruler, the Holy Roman Emperor, and involved many other countries, including Spain, France, Denmark, and Sweden, before it ended in 1648.

Fighting heresy
In this picture the Catholic church is shown as a fortress standing up against Protestantism, which it considered **heresy**. But not all of its methods were violent. By providing better training for priests and encouraging people to become missionaries, the Catholic church also gained many new members at this time.

The Wars of Religion in France
Despite being severely persecuted, by the mid-16th century the Protestants (Huguenots) were an influential group in French politics. This led to the outbreak of civil war in 1562 over who should control the crown. Controlled by his mother, Catherine de' Medici, Charles IX of France ordered the killing of Huguenots on St. Bartholomew's Day in 1572. As many as 20,000 may have died. The pope (right) was so pleased that he held a special service of thanksgiving in Rome.

Henry IV of France
The French Wars of Religion ended with the signing of the Edict of Nantes in 1598, during the reign of Henry IV. He had been a Protestant and a leader of the Huguenots, but became a Catholic in 1593 to secure his position as King of France.

The Edict of Nantes (above) guaranteed religious freedom for French Protestants.

The Inquisition

The Catholic church set up the **Inquisition** to fight heresy. The accused were tortured to make them confess. Those who would not confess were imprisoned or burned to death. The Inquisition was widely used against Protestants in Italy and Spain.

Philip II, king of Spain from 1556 to 1598, saw himself as the champion of the Roman Catholic church in Europe.

Heretics who confessed to their sins had to do a penance or pay a fine to show that they were sorry. Heretics who refused to repent were imprisoned, and sometimes they were marched through the streets wearing tunics decorated with flames (left) before being burned at the stake.

The revolt of the Netherlands

As king of Spain, Philip II also ruled the Netherlands. In 1566 he sent an army to crush the Dutch Protestants, but this provoked a national rebellion. After 18 years of violent struggle, the seven united northern provinces declared their independence.

The Spanish army destroyed Dutch towns, killing entire populations. Left, a mass execution of Protestant rebels.

The Defenestration of Prague

In 1618, Protestant nobles in Bohemia met at Prague to protest against the Holy Roman Emperor's order to pull down their churches. The emperor's officials were thrown out of the window in what became known as the Defenestration of Prague.

The Thirty Years' War (1618–48)

In this war the Protestants were helped by the Netherlands, Denmark, and Sweden – whose king is shown on the left – while Spain helped the Holy Roman Empire. The Protestants won, but only after France fought against the Holy Roman Empire and Spain, despite the fact that all three were Catholic.

SWEDEN
• Novgorod
• Moscow
DENMARK
NETHERLANDS
London •
• Warsaw
• Cologne
• Prague
Paris •
BOHEMIA
Lyons •
Munich • Vienna
Marseilles •
• Venice
• Madrid
Rome •
Constantinople •
SPAIN
Naples •

▨ Anglican   ▨ Lutheran
▨ Calvinist   ▨ Roman Catholic
▨ Eastern Orthodox ▨ Muslim

This map shows how Europe was divided along religious lines by 1700.

Women in the Church

Jesus treated women as equals with men, but the Christian Church has not always done so. Some people believed that, because Eve gave in to temptation in the Garden of Eden, women were somehow inferior to men. Today, however, many branches of the Protestant church treat women equally and allow them to perform **sacraments** just as a man would.

This medieval relief statue shows Eve plucking the apple in the Garden of Eden.

An image of the Virgin Mary is carried through the streets of Warsaw, Poland, in a colorful procession.

This icon from Ethiopia (above) shows Mary by herself and also with the baby Jesus.

Women in the New Testament
The New Testament tells of several women who were important in the early days of the Church. One of the best known is Mary Magdalene, a prostitute who was saved by Jesus and was the first person to speak to him after the Resurrection.

Mary, the mother of Jesus
Mary's importance grew after Jesus died and by the Middle Ages she was second only to Jesus himself. Today she is still very popular in Roman Catholic countries. Pilgrimages and processions are held in her honor (left and below) and people believe she can help them to win God's favor.

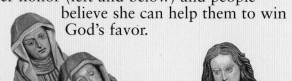

After the Crucifixion, women, including Jesus's mother and Mary Magdalene, prepared his body for burial.

St. Helena and the true cross
St. Helena, mother of the Roman Emperor Constantine, traveled to the Holy Land and founded several churches. Tradition says that she also rediscovered the cross on which Jesus was crucified.

Female saints

Some women were made into saints for their bravery in defending their faith or for their association with Jesus. Others, such as St. Joan and St. Bernadette from France, saw visions of the Virgin Mary that changed their lives completely.

St. Joan of Arc had visions that helped her to lead the French army to victory over the English in 1429 (left).

This miniature (right) shows one of the visions of Hildegard of Bingen, a twelfth century abbess from Germany.

St. Teresa of Avila's visions helped her to reform the Carmelite order of nuns (right).

The separation of women

Some priests believed that people would find it easier to concentrate on the service if men and women sat separately from each other in church (below). The women were also expected to cover their heads.

The legend of Pope Joan

To this day, Catholic priests have been male and unmarried, but in the 13th century the legend of Pope Joan (left) began to circulate. She was well-educated, dressed like a man, and ruled for two years before her secret was discovered when she gave birth to a child while taking part in a procession.

Before the Counter-Reformation, men and women often had to sit separately during sermons and the Mass (above). Sometimes they even had separate entrances to the churches.

Women as ministers

During the late 20th century, women increasingly asked to be given full equality with men in the Church to allow them to hold church services and perform the holy sacraments. They gradually achieved this right in many of the Protestant churches, including the Church of England.

Christianity in the Americas

Christianity first reached the Americas from Europe at the end of the 15th century. Spanish explorers conquered the islands of the West Indies, then Mexico and much of South America, except for Brazil, which was colonized by the Portuguese. Just over a century later, Puritans fleeing from persecution in England brought Christianity to North America when they settled in Massachusetts.

Baroque church in Congonhas, Brazil.

Catholic missionaries

As the French, Spanish, and Portuguese claimed large parts of the Americas, they began to send missionaries from Europe to convert the native population to Catholicism. Spanish influence spread as far north as what are now California, Arizona, New Mexico, and Texas, where some of their mission churches can still be seen today (below).

The Alamo at San Antonio, Texas, was originally built as a missionary church in 1718.

Above: the French friar, Louis Hennepin, was probably the first European to see Niagara Falls.

Above: the native peoples of the Americas worshiped many different gods and goddesses. Quetzalpapalotl (above) was an Aztec god.

Spanish cruelty

When a Spanish missionary called Bartolomeo de las Casas (right) traveled to Cuba in 1513, he was shocked by the atrocities committed on native men, women, children, and babies in the conquest of the country. He wrote detailed reports of what he had seen and publicized them widely when he returned to Spain.

By 1640 there were over 14,000 Puritans in Massachusetts. They were deeply religious and worked hard to make a living.

The Puritans

In 16th century England some people, known as the Puritans, wanted the new Church to be more Protestant. King James I (above) gave in to their demand for a new translation of the Bible in 1612. They still felt persecuted in England, however, and so in September 1620 a group of 102 Puritans left England on a ship called *The Mayflower* to start a new life in North America.

The Mayflower *nears the coast of America in December 1620 (right).*

Converting Native Americans in the north

When the Puritans arrived in Massachusetts, the native population already had its own religion. Some Puritan ministers thought this was uncivilized, however, and tried to convert them to Christianity. John Eliot preached to the Algonquins for 15 years before allowing them into a church.

The Puritans did not tolerate other religions, and in 1660 they hanged Mary Dyer for spreading Quakerism in Massachusetts.

The Quakers

In 1646, the Englishman George Fox had a vision which led him to found the Quakers. Their beliefs were based on love and fellowship, yet they were persecuted in Britain. In 1681 they settled in the state of Pennsylvania. They befriended the Native Americans and insisted on religious tolerance for everyone. This later attracted other religious groups such as the Amish and the Mennonites.

The Quakers were also called the Religious Society of Friends. They dressed plainly and addressed each other as "thee" and "thou," instead of "you."

The Seven Sacraments

The seven sacraments are solemn rituals which help to bring God's blessing to an individual or a group of people. The central rituals are the Eucharist and baptism, and these are accepted by all branches of the Christian Church. The other five are confirmation, confession, holy matrimony, holy orders, and anointing the sick.

The Eucharist

The Eucharist, in which the priest gives consecrated bread and wine (or grape juice) to the congregation, is the most important sacrament in the Christian Church. Also known as Mass or Communion, it has its origins in the Last Supper, when Jesus shared bread and wine with his Disciples. The bread represents his body and the wine represents the blood he shed for his followers.

Baptism

Baptism is the first sacrament of the Christian Church, and it often takes place shortly after a child is born. A priest or minister pours water over the child's forehead, welcoming him or her into the Christian Church and giving the child his or her name.

The First Communion, for which all the girls dress in white, is a highlight of Roman Catholic childhood.

Some Christian groups believe in adult baptism, with total immersion in water.

Confirmation

Confirmation is the ceremony that makes a person a full member of the Church, and it usually allows them to join in the Eucharist. It can take place in childhood, adolescence, or adulthood. Not all Christian churches observe confirmation.

Holy Matrimony

The sacrament of Holy Matrimony, or marriage, takes place in front of a priest or minister. During the ceremony, the bride and groom promise to be faithful to each other until death. Marriage also symbolizes the union between Jesus and his Church.

Church weddings are still popular, even though there are now many alternatives.

Confession

Confession is important in the Roman Catholic church, where priests are able to listen to confessions of wrongdoing and to forgive the confessor in the name of God.

Holy Orders

The sacrament of Holy Orders is the ceremony by which the status of priesthood is conferred on someone by a bishop, usually after several years of study and training. Roman Catholic priests often wear special clothes, or vestments, like these on the right, when they officiate at services.

When a Christian is dying, like this man in the Middle Ages (below), he or she will often confess his or her sins in the hope of going to Heaven.

The Ten Commandments

As well as the teachings of Jesus, Christians try to obey the Ten Commandments. The Old Testament tells us that these were carved on tablets of stone given by God to Moses as he led his people out of Egypt.

Anointing the sick

Many branches of the Church have services to help the sick and the dying. They include saying special prayers and the laying on of hands. Those who are very sick can be blessed and anointed with holy oil in preparation for death.

Service to others

At the Last Supper, Jesus washed the dust from the road off of his Disciples' feet, probably in a bowl like the one on the left. As this was a task usually performed by servants, Jesus did it to show his followers that they must go out and serve others as he had served them.

Churches Around the World

Between 1500 and 1900 a handful of European countries gradually took control over large parts of the world. At first these countries–Spain, Portugal, Britain, France, and the Netherlands–were mainly interested in trade, but then they began to build up empires for themselves in Africa, America, and much of Asia. As their colonies became firmly established, each country sent its missionaries to convert the local people to Christianity.

Missionaries in Africa

Missionaries, as shown on this carving from Nigeria (above), believed they were helping the Africans by introducing them to Christianity. They were among the first Europeans to travel beyond the coast of their continent. Eventually they set up schools as well as churches.

Cardinal Lavigerie

Cardinal Lavigerie (left) was archbishop of Algiers, and in 1868 he founded the White Fathers Missionary Society to convert Africans to Christianity. He also had a social conscience and spent his later years organizing antislavery societies to protect the people of central Africa.

Map showing the routes of the main missionary journeys to Africa.

Ancient Coptic tapestry made of linen and wool.

The Coptic Orthodox church

The Coptic Orthodox church is the main Christian church in Egypt. The Copts, a minority religious group in predominantly Muslim Egypt, use Arabic in their services.

Above: a priest from the Ethiopian Orthodox church. Ethiopia is the only country in northern Africa where most people are Christians.

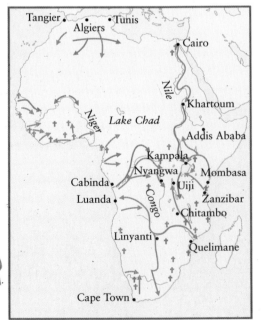

† Protestant missions
† Roman Catholic missions
→ Advance of Protestant missions
→ Advance of Roman Catholic missions

An image of the Virgin Mary is carried in this Roman Catholic procession at Pondicherry in India.

Christianity in India

The Indian subcontinent already had well-established religions of its own when the Europeans arrived. The majority of people were either Hindus or Muslims, but there were also Sikhs and Buddhists in many areas. In spite of this, Portuguese missionaries converted some people to Roman Catholicism in their colonies, while Dutch and British missionaries converted some people to Protestantism.

Christianity in Japan

In 1549 a Spanish priest went to Japan and started converting people to Roman Catholicism. Others missionaries followed and by 1600 they had converted around 300,000 people. The ruler of Japan then thought foreign armies would follow the missionaries, so he threw them all out and told the Japanese converts (below) to give up their new religion or be killed.

Converting Africans in the US

During the 17th to 19th centuries, many millions of Africans were taken from their homelands and sold into slavery in the US. They had their own religions, but their owners brought in preachers to convert them to Christianity.

Voodoo, practiced in parts of the Caribbean, is a mixture of West African and Catholic beliefs. Trances, drumming, and dancing are important parts of the rituals.

Left: sometimes religions intermingle, as on this Christian cross with a statue of Buddha in the center.

This statue of the Madonna and Child is from the Solomon Islands in the Pacific Ocean.

Christianity reaches all parts of the world

By the late 20th century, Christianity had reached all parts of the world, including remote islands in the Pacific, Indian, and Atlantic oceans. In many places, however, its followers were few, and missionaries concentrated more on education and health care rather than trying to convert large numbers of people.

Feast Days

The most important Christian feast days are Christmas and **Easter**, when people remember Jesus's birth and his death. Christmas is always on December 25, but Easter Sunday can be on any date between March 22 and April 25 as it is always on the first Sunday after the first full moon after the Spring Equinox (March 21). The dates for Lent, Palm Sunday, Pentecost, and Ascension Day are set by the date of Easter each year.

No one knew the exact date of Jesus's birth, but December 25 was chosen in 336.

Epiphany

The Feast of the Epiphany on January 6 remembers the day when the three Wise Men arrived with their gifts for the baby Jesus. In some countries gifts are exchanged then rather than at Christmas, while in Germany children dress up as kings.

Lent and Mardi Gras

Lent is the 40 days before Easter, starting with Ash Wednesday, when Christians were supposed to fast and do penance for their sins. The day before Lent is Mardi Gras or Fat Tuesday, and is marked with carnivals in many places, including Rio de Janeiro and Venice.

On Fridays and during Lent, Christians could eat fish but not meat. This was to remind them of Jesus's time of fasting in the wilderness.

When Jesus rode into Jerusalem on the Sunday before Easter, people threw palm leaves in his path. Palm Sunday commemorates this event.

Holy Week

Holy Week is the time between Palm Sunday and Easter Sunday, when Christians remember the events leading up to Jesus's death and Resurrection. In southern Spain it is marked by processions of penitents (people who are sorry for the sins they have committed) carrying crosses and wearing long robes and tall pointed hats (left).

Maundy Thursday is the day when Christians remember Jesus's Last Supper with his disciples.

Good Friday and Easter Sunday

Good Friday is the most solemn day in the Christian year as people remember Jesus's death. Many places mark the event with a procession. In contrast, Easter Sunday is the most joyous day and churches are decorated with flowers as people remember Jesus's Resurrection.

Eggs are traditional pagan symbols of revival and new life, associated with spring festivals. Christians often eat decorated or chocolate eggs on Easter Sunday as a reminder of Christ's Resurrection.

Hot cross buns and simnel cake are eaten at Easter. In Germany pretzels are popular.

Other Feast Days and Saints' Days

There are many more feast days in the Christian year. They include Ascension Day, which is 40 days after Easter and commemorates Jesus's ascent into Heaven, Whitsuntide (below left) on the seventh Sunday after Easter, and Assumption Day on August 15, celebrating Mary's ascent into Heaven (right). Many saints also have their own days; All Saints' Day celebrates all of them.

Pentecost, or Whitsuntide, celebrates the day when Jesus's disciples received the Holy Spirit.

The Day of the Dead

November 2 is All Souls' Day, or the Day of the Dead, and it commemorates all Christians who have died. In many countries people place lighted candles on the graves of their friends and relatives, while in Mexico people make skulls from candy for the children to eat (right).

41

Christianity Today

At the start of the 21st century, there is a greater mix of religions in the world than there used to be, but Christianity continues to expand and gain new followers. In the USA especially, evangelists on stage and television convert new members at every appearance, while in the former communist countries of eastern Europe the Church has quickly re-established itself, often helped by Christian groups from other parts of the world.

Karol Wojtyla, a Pole, became Pope John Paul II in 1978. By traveling widely, he won greater support for Roman Catholicism.

Charity work

In the 20th century, many Christian organizations became involved in charity work. One of the best-known is the Order of the Missionaries of Charity, founded by Mother Teresa (left) to work among the very poor, especially in India. She died in 1997, but her work continues.

"The Sons of God"

Some missionaries today are very different from those of earlier centuries. For example, in the USA a group known as the "Sons of God" is made up of former Hell's Angels. Dressed like bikers themselves, they go to Christian rallies to try and spread the Christian message among the bikers who attend.

Millions of Christians from around the world flocked to Italy to take part in the Jubilee in the year 2000. A Roman Catholic priest in Florence, Italy, welcomes a young woman in a wheelchair.

Working for social justice

Some recent Christian leaders have used their position to try and bring about more social justice and better conditions for the people who follow them. For example, Desmond Tutu played a major role in the abolishment of apartheid in South Africa, while Martin Luther King won the Nobel Peace prize for his non-violent campaign for Black civil rights in the US.

The Rev Martin Luther King was assassinated in 1968.

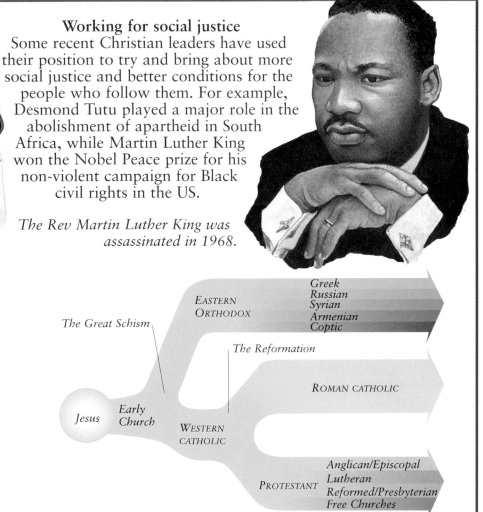

Northern Ireland

British soldiers have patrolled the streets of Northern Ireland for over 30 years, trying to stop a dispute developing into a full-scale war between the Roman Catholic minority who want Ireland to be reunited into one country and the Protestant majority who want it to remain part of the United Kingdom. A peace agreement signed in 1998 has improved matters, however.

The Salvation Army is an international Christian religious and charity movement organized and run on military lines.

EASTERN ORTHODOX
Greek
Russian
Syrian
Armenian
Coptic

The Great Schism

The Reformation

ROMAN CATHOLIC

Jesus — Early Church

WESTERN CATHOLIC

PROTESTANT
Anglican/Episcopal
Lutheran
Reformed/Presbyterian
Free Churches

Christian diversity

There have always been different Christian groups that believe different answers to questions such as how to describe Jesus, or the best way to worship God. There are many different traditions of Christianity in the world today, and new churches are still being founded by people with new ideas.

About eight percent of the population of Taiwan is Christian. This Taiwanese couple was married according to Christian rites.

GLOSSARY

Apostles: The closest followers of Jesus during his life on Earth. The Twelve Apostles are also known as the Twelve Disciples.

Baptism: The ceremony which brings people into the Christian faith by the use of water for immersion or sprinkling, and the recital of holy words.

Bible: Christianity's most sacred book. It was written between about 1000 BCE and 100 CE and is made up of many different books. It is divided into the Old and the New Testaments.

Cathedral: A church that contains a cathedra, a throne for a bishop, and that is officially the principal church of a diocese, a district over which the bishop has authority.

Christ: The Greek word for one who is accepted as the Messiah, or Anointed One. Both Christ and the Messiah are other names for Jesus in Christianity.

Christianity: The religion based on the life, teachings, and death of Jesus Christ.

Church, the Church: The word "church" has two different meanings to Christians. Originally "the Church" was used to describe the whole community of Christians throughout the world. As Christianity grew in popularity, the word "church" was also used to describe the buildings in which Christians met to worship and pray. The word is also now used to describe the different sects within Christianity (the Orthodox church, the Roman Catholic church, etc.)

Confirmation: The ceremony that makes a person a full member of the Church.

Convert: To persuade a person to follow a particular religious faith.

Cross: Two pieces of wood that are fastened together, from which a person is hung as a means of execution. Jesus died on a Roman cross, and his death by this means is called the Crucifixion. The cross is now the symbol of Christianity.

Crusades: Military attacks launched against non-Christians by the pope in 1095, which continued for three centuries.

Easter: The annual Christian festival that celebrates Christ's Resurrection. Easter Sunday is celebrated on the first Sunday after the first full moon after the Spring Equinox.

Gospels: The Gospels are the story of Christ's life and teachings contained in the first four books in the New Testament of the Bible. The term "gospel" is also used to describe the Christian faith and the teachings of Jesus and the Apostles as a whole.

Great Schism: A state of divided spiritual allegiance in Christianity caused by a disputed papal election, particularly the period between 1378 and 1417, when there were rival popes in Rome and Avignon.

Heresy: Adherence to opinions or beliefs that are contrary to the dominant belief. A person who holds these contrary beliefs is called a heretic.

Hermit: A person who lives in complete solitude in order to practice religious exercises.

Holy Land: The land associated with Jesus while he was alive, and associated with places from the Bible.

Holy Roman Empire: An empire established in 800 CE, when Pope Leo III crowned king Charlemagne, a supporter of Christianity, emperor over a vast area of Europe.

Holy Spirit: The active presence of God in human life, also called the Holy Ghost. One part of the Holy Trinity.

Holy Trinity: One God composed of three separate but equal persons: God the Father, God the Son, and the Holy Spirit.

Icon: A sacred image depicting Christ, the Virgin Mary, a saint, or some other religious subject, revered in churches and homes.

Inquisition: A Catholic seat of judgement created in Spain in medieval and early modern times to investigate heresy and stop it with harsh punishment.

Judaism: The religion of the Jews characterized by belief in one God and adherence to the Hebrew Scriptures.

Last Supper: The last time Jesus and his Apostles ate together, on the Jewish feast of Passover.

Madonna: A picture, statue, or other representation of the Virgin Mary, Christ's mother.

Magi: The three Wise Men from the East who paid homage to the infant Jesus soon after his birth. Each year the feast of the Epiphany is celebrated on January 6, the day of their visit.

Mass: The Christian sacrament in which a priest gives sacred bread and wine to the congregation, in honor of Jesus's sharing of bread and wine with his Apostles at the Last Supper. Also known as Holy Communion or the Eucharist.

Mission: An institution created by a church to convert people to a religion, particularly Christianity. Those who travel to create missions are called missionaries.

Monastery: A house of religious seclusion from the world, for people who have taken vows to lead a life devoted to religion. The men who live in monasteries are known as monks, while women leading monastic lives are known as nuns. Nuns live in convents.

Pilgrim: A person who travels to visit a holy place. A journey undertaken by a pilgrim is known as a pilgrimage.

Pope: The leader of the Roman Catholic church, also known as the Bishop of Rome.

Protestant: A Christian who does not adhere to the faith of the Roman Catholic or Eastern churches. Also used to describe the church or faith of such a person. Protestant faith grew out of the Reformation of the 16th century.

Reformation: A 16th-century religious movement aimed at correcting corruption within the Roman Catholic church, and marked ultimately by the rejection of the supremacy of the pope, the modification of Roman Catholic practices, and the creation of Protestant churches. It was followed in 1545 by the Counter-Reformation, a movement started by Pope Paul III aimed at improving the Roman Catholic church from within.

Resurrection: The act of Jesus Christ's rising to life from the dead, three days after his death on the cross. The Resurrection is celebrated each year at Easter.

Saint: A holy person officially honored after death in the Church for piety during life. A patron saint is a special guardian in Heaven who protects the interests of a group, activity, or country.

Sacrament: A solemn ritual in the Christian church which helps to bring God's blessing to an individual or group of people.

Ten Commandments: Ten instructions for life given by God to Moses which all Christians must follow. Also known as the Decalogue.

INDEX

Acknowledgements

The Publishers would like to thank the following photographers and picture libraries for the photos used in this book.

t=top; tl=top left; tc=top center; tr=top right; c=center; cl=center left; b=bottom; bl=bottom left; bc=bottom center; br=bottom right

Cover Index/Cantarelli; **9b** Press Photo, Florence; **10tl** Accademia, Florence/Scala Group; **21tc**The Bridgeman Art Library/Overseas; **33c** Scala Group; **37tl** Chuck Savage/Stock Market International; **40bc** Marco Lanza; **41tr** Museo di San Marco, Florence/Scala Group; **42bl** Press Photo, Florence; **43br** Marco Nardi/McRae Books Archives